ALL YEAR ROUND

Autumn

Susan Humphries

Based on the Central television programmes

Macdonald Educational

HOW TO USE THIS BOOK

First, look at the contents page opposite. The chapter list tells you what each page is about.

If you want to know about one particular thing, look it up in the index on page 30. For example, if you want to know about blood, the index tells you that there is something about it on pages 14 and 18. The index also lists the pictures in the book.

When you read this book, you will find some unusual words. The glossary on pages 28–29 explains what they mean.

Editor
Claire Llewellyn

Series design
Liz Black

Book design
Sylvia Tate

Production
Marguerite Fenn

Picture research
Diana Morris

Factual adviser
M G Ayres

Teacher panel
Mary Gribbin
Jules Steel

The poem on page 19 is included with the kind permission of the Literary Trustees of Walter de la Mare and the Society of Authors as their representative.

Illustrations
Graham Allen: 6
Clare Barber: 19
Peter Bull: 10 (top), 20 (bottom), 22 (top), 23 (top)
Robert Morton: 14, 26, 27
Cynthia Pow: 7 (bottom), 8 (top), 12 (top), 15 (top), 16
John Rignall: 9, 10 (bottom), 11 (top)
Kate Rogers: 7 (top), 15 (bottom), 17 (top), 18, 23 (bottom), 24, 25
Larry Ronstadt: front cover
Sylvia Tate: 8 (bottom), 11 (bottom), 12 (bottom), 17 (bottom), 20 (top)

Photographs
Barnaby's: 24
Sally & Richard Greenhill: 14, 22
Eric & David Hosking: 26
O.S.F.: 13 (bottom)
Zefa: 6, 13 (top), 21

CONTENTS

HARVESTING	6–13
Harvesting is the gathering in	6–7
Plants and seeds	8–9
You can make your own harvest	10–11
An all year round activity	12–13

FEEDING	14–21
Why do we need food?	14–15
Eating for health	16–17
Inside and out	18
'Miss T': poem	19
Food is . . . variety!	20–21

FAMILIES	22–27
Joining a family	22–23
Belonging	24–25
Animal families	26–27

GLOSSARY	28–29
INDEX	30
NOTES FOR ADULTS	31

HARVESTING

Harvesting is the gathering in

Harvesting is the gathering in of all the things we need: from the soil, from the sea, from underground.
When trees are cut down, we harvest wood.
We also harvest things people make.

From underground mines we harvest coal.

Farmers provide us with food. They cultivate land to grow grain and root crops.

Some harvests are gathered by hand, such as flowers, pears, rhubarb and melons. Have you ever picked fruit or flowers? Produce grown in market gardens is usually gathered by hand, too.

You can grow and harvest your own crops. Get some help from an adult to buy a packet of seeds. Follow the instructions on the packet. You could sow the seeds in a garden if the weather is warm, or grow them in a pot indoors.

Have you ever picked apples from a tree, or blackberries from a bush?

Do not overwater indoor plants

25cm

To grow potatoes, plant a seed potato in a deep pot.

10cm

Alfalfa is a leaf crop and grows from seed.

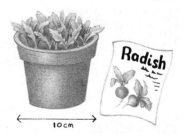

10cm

Radish is a root crop. It is good in salad.

Plants produce roots, leaves, stalks, flowers and seeds as part of their natural growth. Sometimes we can use nearly all the plant, but mostly we use just one part.

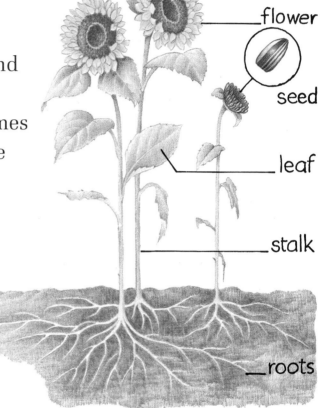

flower

seed

leaf

stalk

roots

Can you name the parts of these plants which we harvest?

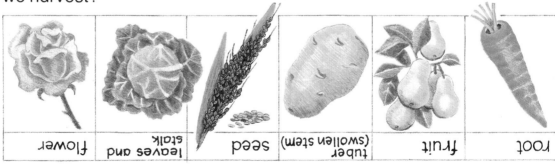

| flower | leaves and stalk | seed | tuber (swollen stem) | fruit | root |

We always save some seeds from the
harvested crop for future planting.
We can then grow the same crop next year.

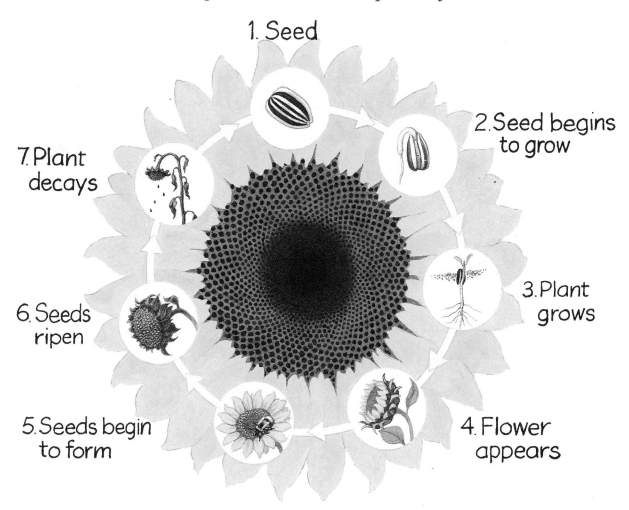

1. Seed

2. Seed begins to grow

3. Plant grows

4. Flower appears

5. Seeds begin to form

6. Seeds ripen

7. Plant decays

This is the seed-to-seed cycle of a sunflower.

A mature sunflower head has a beautiful
pattern of seeds in the centre. If you store some
ripe seeds you can plant them in the spring or
give them to birds in the winter.
We harvest sunflowers for the oil in their seeds.

HARVESTING

You can make your own harvest

Thousands of years ago, people made the discovery that certain kinds of wild grass, such as wheat, had seeds which could be crushed to get flour. When the flour was mixed with water and cooked, it made a simple bread.

Put some seeds on a piece of cloth.

Crush the seeds with a stone.

What have you made?

Later, people discovered that if they cleared the ground and planted seeds from the last harvest, they did not have to search for new seeds. Each autumn people saved the best seeds to store and plant in the following spring. It was the start of growing crops for food and the first kind of farming.

Have you ever picked a bunch of wild grasses? Try it. In the summer months, look along the edge of a field, a hedge or a fence. Find grass stalks with a head of seeds. Look at them closely. How many different grasses have you found? What is different about them? Are the seeds the same? You can make a book of grasses.

Your mounted collection of grasses and seeds will be your own herbarium.

Most of the flour we use today for making bread is from wheat. Other kinds of flour are produced from maize, barley, oats and rye. All of these flour-producing seeds are from the grass family. Rice is also a member of the grass family. Grasses provide us with more food than any other plant family.

What things do you eat that are made with flour?

HARVESTING

An all year round activity

Plants grow and ripen at different rates and in different seasons. We harvest plants when they have most value to us. We gather vegetables before they get too old. When are apples ready to pick?

We pick flowers in bud or in bloom, before they seed.

If we want a good harvest from our crops, we must take care of them while they are growing. Every type of plant needs a different kind of care. How is growing plums different from growing wheat? Think of some reasons why a harvest might fail. What would happen if a grain harvest did fail?

How do these things affect a healthy plant?

Because the grain harvest is so important, we celebrate in the autumn after it has been gathered in. We call this Harvest Festival.

Dancers from Japan are celebrating the harvest.

People all over the world celebrate the successful harvest of grain crops.

These bees are making their own harvest of honey.

Throughout the year people all over the world are harvesting food, fuel, minerals and ideas.

FEEDING

Why do we need food?

Are you alive? How do you know? Dead things are very still. They do not move.
They do not eat.
They do not breathe.
They are still all over.

Is this rabbit dead or asleep?

We know we are alive because, even when we are resting or sleeping, our heart is beating, sending blood through our bodies; our lungs expand and contract as we breathe air; we get hungry and need food. Food gives us energy.

We need energy to stay awake, to move, to think.

14

Food helps us to grow. Food helps us to keep healthy. Plants are living things too; they need food and water from the soil. Sometimes we feed the soil with manure or with chemical fertilizer. A plant's roots absorb this food from the soil.

A plant makes food from the sun's energy and also gathers it from the soil.

What we eat is called our diet. We need different kinds of foods for a balanced diet.
In every country the food is a little different.

We eat different kinds of food in all manner of ways.

FEEDING

Eating for health

1.

All these things are made from milk.

2.

These plants and plant seed cases can be eaten.

A balanced diet means eating foods from five important food groups. This will help your body get what it needs to keep healthy. Think about your diet. How can you improve it? Fresh foods are delicious and those you can eat without cooking are very good for you. All of us need vitamins, minerals, protein, fibre, fats and carbohydrates; there are small amounts of these things in most food.

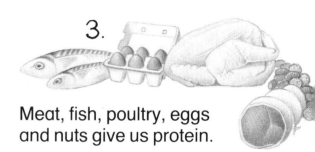

3.

Meat, fish, poultry, eggs and nuts give us protein.

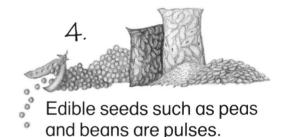

4.

Edible seeds such as peas and beans are pulses.

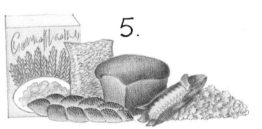

5.

Cereals give us another kind of seed.

If you could choose your favourite food today,
what would you put on these plates,
and in the lunch box and glasses?

for breakfast   for lunch   for tea

Check your chosen foods and see if you can
find which food group they belong to. What
would happen if you ate your favourite food
every single day for a year? Remember: if you
fill up with biscuits, crisps and sweets you
will not get all the things your body needs.

Which three of these would you choose for a
balanced diet? What would be a healthy snack?

FEEDING

Inside and out

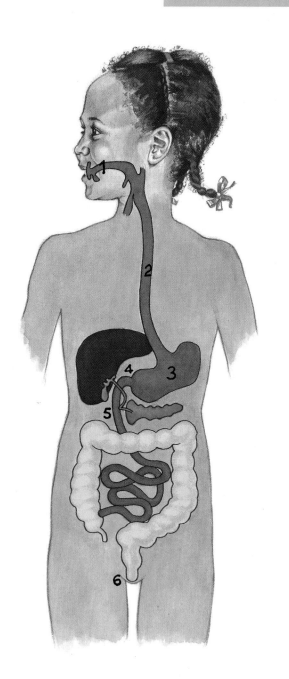

Do you know what happens to food inside your body? (1) Your teeth grind up food and mix it with saliva. This makes it easier to swallow. (2) The food is squeezed down into your stomach through your food pipe. (3) Special juices in your stomach start to change the food into a thick liquid. (4) A special valve lets the food through into your small intestine. (5) In the small intestine more juices help to dissolve the food. The useful food travels through your body in your blood. (6) The bits of food which are not useful leave your body when you go to the toilet.

Miss T

It's a very odd thing –
As odd as can be –
That whatever Miss T eats
Turns into Miss T;
Porridge and apples,
Mince, muffins and mutton
Jam, junket, jumbles –
Not a rap, nor a button
It matters; the moment
they're out of her plate,
Though shared by Miss Butcher
And sour Mr Bate:
Tiny and cheerful
And neat as can be,
Whatever Miss T eats
Turns into Miss T.

Walter de la Mare

FEEDING

Food is . . . variety!

Food has a smell and a taste. Name one salty food you like, then a sweet one, then a fruity one and then a sour one. Eating can be an adventure! Can you invent a new sandwich or help cook a new recipe?

Read the labels on packets and tins. Which countries did this food come from?

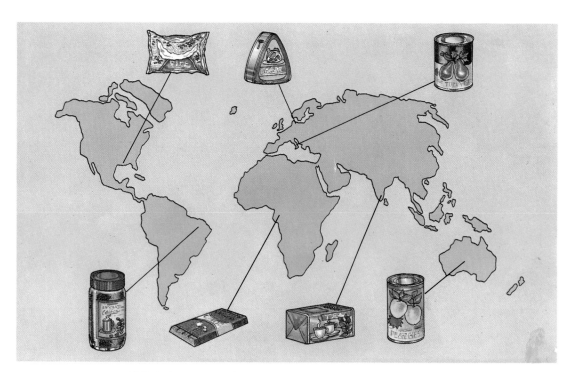

Which countries produced these foods?

Food comes to us from countries all over the world. This makes our diet interesting and full of variety. Years ago, you could only eat what was grown locally because fresh food went bad on long journeys. Can you name some ways of keeping food fresh?

Animals do not cook their food. Make a zoo tea for yourself and a friend. Use raw food such as chopped carrot, honey, nuts and sunflower seeds. Meals are fun if they are shared. Families and friends get together to eat at happy or sad times.

It is important to eat with friends and family.

FAMILIES
Joining a family

Every family is special.
No two families can ever be
the same. That is what
makes your family special.
Mum and Dad do not always
live in the same house. Who
lives with you? When do you
have most fun together?
When are you all cross?

Think of your family in this
picture frame.

How do you help your family?

How do they help you?

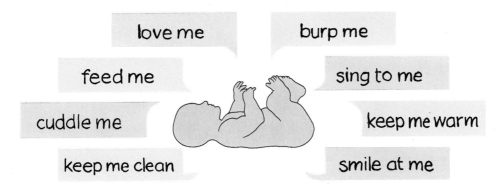

love me

burp me

feed me

sing to me

cuddle me

keep me warm

keep me clean

smile at me

When a human baby is born it is helpless.

A new baby depends on other humans to look after it. We look after its body by changing its nappy, bathing it, feeding it and keeping it warm. We also cuddle the baby and we smile, sing and talk to it to show that we love it.

The people living with the baby and looking after it are usually the baby's close family. As a baby grows, it does more things for itself. It copies people and tries to please those it loves.

It smiles, tries to walk, uses a potty and learns to share.

FAMILIES

Belonging

These are families. How are they different?
How are they the same?

Relations and friends are a part of your
family too. A baby belongs to all these people
and learns to know them and return their love.

Did this family live together in the same house?

As we grow up, we get to know more people.
We join groups to do all kinds of things.

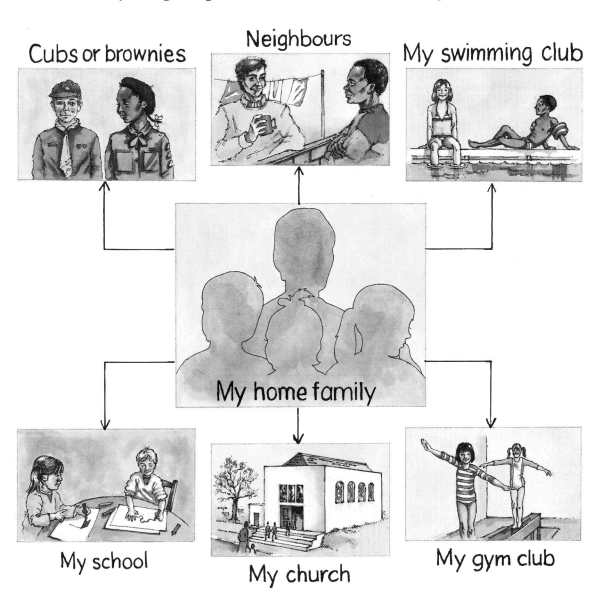

Cubs or brownies

Neighbours

My swimming club

My home family

My school

My church

My gym club

We all belong to several groups of people.
They are also like families for us. We make
friends who become very important to us.

FAMILIES
Animal families

You know your own family. Did you know that some other animals have families too? They live with their families until they are old enough to live by themselves. Later they will start new families.

How does a bird's life begin?

Some animals live in family groups all their lives. They work together, protect each other, and help to keep the young ones safe.

These animals live in a family group.

All living things change. Look back to page 9. Do you remember the seed-to-seed cycle? Here is another cycle. This shows how foxes live.

This is a year cycle in the life of an adult fox.

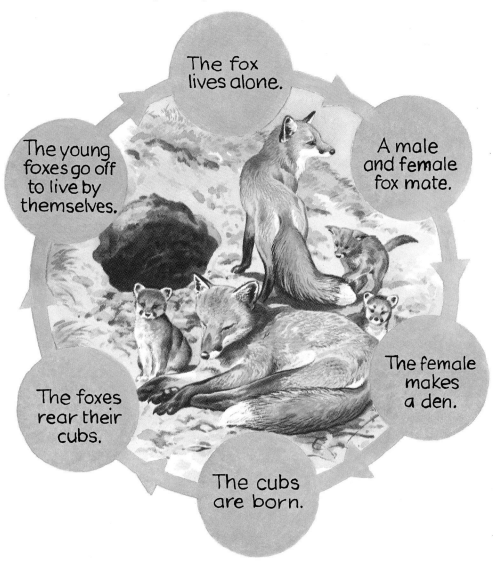

The fox lives alone.

The young foxes go off to live by themselves.

A male and female fox mate.

The foxes rear their cubs.

The female makes a den.

The cubs are born.

GLOSSARY

carbohydrate	One of the substances found in a food like bread. It gives us energy.
cycle	Things which happen again and again in a regular pattern, like the seasons of the year.
diet	The food we eat on a day-by-day basis.
edible	If something is edible, it means we can eat it.
energy	When we have energy we are full of life and can do a lot of work.
fats	The oily part of a plant or animal.
fertilizer	Something which is added to the soil to make it richer, so that plants grow better.

fibre	The bulky part of food which we need to help food move from one part of our body to another.
fuel	Something we can burn to produce heat.
grain	The seeds of cereal plants.
manure	The droppings of animals mixed with straw.
mineral	A substance in food which our body needs to work properly.
protein	A substance in food which our body needs to help us grow and stay healthy.
saliva	A liquid in the mouth which starts to break down the food we eat.
vitamin	This is a part of food our body needs in tiny amounts to stay healthy.

INDEX

The **dark** numbers show you where there is a picture of the subject.

Bb
blood 14, 18

Cc
carbohydrates 16, 28
cereals **16**, 29
crops **6**, 7, **7**, 9, 10, 12

Dd
diet 15, 16, **17**, 21, 28

Ee
energy 14, **14**, 15, 28

Ff
fertilizer 15, 28
food **6**, 10, 11, 13, 14, 15, **15**, 16, **16**, **17**, 18, 20, **20**, 21, 28, 29

Hh
harvesting 6, **6**, 7, **8**, 9, 10, 12, 13, **13**
herbarium **11**

Mm
minerals 13, 16, 29

Pp
plants 8, **8**, 11, 12, **12**, 15, **15**, **16**, 28
protein 16, **16**, 29

Rr
roots **6**, **7**, 8, **8**, 15

Ss
saliva 18, 29
seeds 7, **7**, 8, 9, **9**, 10, **10**, 11, **11**, **12**, **16**, 21
seed-to-seed cycle **9**, 27
smell 20
soil 6, 15, **15**, 28

Tt
taste 20

Vv
vitamins 16, 29

Yy
year cycle 27, **27**